Sublimity

The Power to Inspire

AF665028

Deepti Belliappa Ganapathy

BookLeaf Publishing
India | USA | UK

Copyright © Deepti Belliappa Ganapathy
All Rights Reserved.

This book has been self-published with all reasonable efforts taken to make the material error-free by the author. No part of this book shall be used, reproduced in any manner whatsoever without written permission from the author, except in the case of brief quotations embodied in critical articles and reviews.
The Author of this book is solely responsible and liable for its content including but not limited to the views, representations, descriptions, statements, information, opinions, and references ["Content"]. The Content of this book shall not constitute or be construed or deemed to reflect the opinion or expression of the Publisher or Editor. Neither the Publisher nor Editor endorse or approve the Content of this book or guarantee the reliability, accuracy, or completeness of the Content published herein and do not make any representations or warranties of any kind, express or implied, including but not limited to the implied warranties of merchantability, fitness for a particular purpose.
The Publisher and Editor shall not be liable whatsoever...

Made with ❤ on the BookLeaf Publishing Platform
www.bookleafpub.in
www.bookleafpub.com

To everyone who values what it means to be 'beautiful' inside out!

Cherishing the magic in every walk of life.

Acknowledgement

With love and thanks to my parents, brother, husband and children for their enduring patience and for being a part of my life journey as I continue to grow as a person.

I am grateful to my professional community who has given me the confidence of seeing inspiration in everything around us and giving me my wings to ink from my heart.

I am deeply grateful to my family and friends who have stood by me with their unwavering support and honest guidance always.

I acknowledge the support of the team at BookLeaf Publishing who has worked with me tirelessly to bring this book to its fruition.

Preface

'Sublimity is the echo of the noble mind' (Longinus) - Beautiful is seen as limited but being sublime is perceived as limitless. The mind often tries to imagine what is beyond its calibre. The same mind in sublimity experiences heartbreak during failure and immense happiness at the very attempt of attaining this.

In the words of Buddha:
What you think you become,
What you feel, you attract,
What you imagine, you create!

This book is a compilation of poems that have a shade of sublimity to each of them. As you delve into each line, you will see the value in small things that shape our reality and blend the many emotions that make our being. The fragility of life is inexplicable and this poetic journey is a gentle reminder of a marriage between our past, present, and the future.

Preface

TABLE OF CONTENTS

I. Dear Reader

'A reader lives a thousand lives before he dies.'
— George RR Martin

'Poetry must be read to be poetry.
It may be that one reader is all I deserve.
If this is so, I want that reader to be you!'
—William Saroyan

As I write the topic, I smile and think,
Compiling these lines for my dear reader to link!
When you write for your soul, your core feels crisper,
When you write for your heart, your dear readers hear your whispers.

As I string these words to share a poetic tale,
For you dear reader, I yearn not to fail.
The captivating scenery or the loyal pet fills the heart,
The battling emotions or losses that matter is another part!

There are vivid images that I have made,
A visual treat for you is what I prayed!
There will be lines which inspire you for more,
It's a poetic journey dear reader, to liven your core.

Every page has something from my life,
There are captures that show you even shades of strife.
Just like life, there are both sides to the play,
Balancing this art, dear reader, is your challenge every day.

So as you embark on this poetic journey with me,
Exceeding your expectations, I yearn, but it's no guarantee.
Dear reader seek your connection with the hopes I have shaped,
Learn from my mistakes, so much heartbreak can be escaped.

With patience, you have walked this journey with me,
In many ways, you have inspired the words that you see.
I am grateful for being my dear reader with that feedback and applause,
You give me motivation to give wings to an everyday cause.

II. Sublimity - Seeking the inspiration

'Know how sublime a thing it is to suffer and be strong.' — Henry Wadsworth Longfellow

The words are weaved together, there is depth for you,
The imagery is vivid, the message is for you to construe.
Emotions have been blended into small insights from me,
The message is there, embrace this true sublimity.

Every page is a canvas of reflections and hope,
The complex human stance has so much to cope;
By drawing parallels to the landscape around us,
Find your sublimity in this compilation, a worthy discuss!

Shades of hope, imagination, and dreams we see,
With the signs of times blended into the minds of older and younger me.
Choices to make or the fear of rejection grip my heart,
The momentary applause and the eulogy I will miss, have another part.

Life has much to offer with charm,
Draw the inspirations that keep your calm.
The sublimity of this tapestry of life that we weave,
Treasured in our hands to keep is what I believe.

The beauty in something so small, yet the grandness we call,
There is silence in sublimity in our daily grind, big or small.
While the beauty around us tickles the senses to come alive,
True sublimity confides in our mind, a reason to thrive.

III. Hope

'Once you choose hope, anything is possible'
— Christopher Reeve

The blue sea speaks to me,
In soft whispers I feel calm till eternity.
I hope for peace in spite of the hustle around,
It's a tranquillity that is often hard to be
found!

In my heart, I have him wrapped up tight,
Walks on four but loves with all his might.
I hoped he spoke with actions and words to me,
A lifetime unspoken, this fur baby's heart will be free.

I often wonder about the kindred spirits from the past,
Always hoped those equations in this lifetime would last.
I hoped that they appeared in front of my door,
To embrace the family I made and even the missing score.

The incomplete conversions with the estranged friend,
Will always be a hope for us to mend.
I always hope that equations see the emotions without any pride,
The world would be cherishing a memorable ride.

So many scenarios for us to hope,
A world free of strife and disparity, so much
to cope!
I dream of being in a world free from
conditions and fear,
The doctrine of life will be definitely clear.

IV. Bond Beyond Words

'Stick with the people who pull the magic out of you, not the madness'. — Unknown

Time has gone by but it feels like yesterday,
From the little giggles to now chasing life troubles away.
The stones that we piled for our games back then,
Have been our innocent memories that can't be forgotten!

Many milestones we have seen,
In each other's lives from a princess to a queen.
Now at the brim of growing pains and aches,
The challenges are more, yet our friendship tides any breaks.

The routine flusters often seeking a quick respite for sure,
The hearty conversations over a coffee, bring much cheer.
There are times when I fail in every role,
But not being judged in this friendship is the true goal.

With confidence I know, my thoughts are shared,
Secrets well kept, that no one dared.
Promises to be dependable and patient I know,
Expectations are not measured in this role to grow.

It's not the connection by blood or distance here,
There is comfort, respect and a shoulder for the tear.
Time is not the essence of this friendship neither is familiarity,
Some equations redefine its strength to eternity.

The biggest blessing is, knowing you are there,
Without an everyday reminder that I care!
Just an occasional message or a quick hello may seem,
My reason to smile when reality bursts life's dreams!

Hand in hand, know that I care,
Friends like family are very rare.
Thank you for being there any time for sure,
These rare 3 am friends are an all-round cure.

V. The Happiness Jar

'There is no way to happiness. Happiness is the way.' —Thich Nhat Hanh

Sitting on the shelf in my room I see it there,
Labelled as the happiness jar, it holds my
happiness to share.
Every time my heart smiles from deep within,
A colourful note would be dropped,
celebrating a life win.

The prom party at school was a memory here,
Graduating from school and college was an incomparable cheer.
Gifting my mother with diamonds from an early earning,
Fills my heart with memories worth returning!

Marriage and the family growing with the kids had much thrill,
Amidst the chaos and mundane life drill;
Milestones have been many, recorded with coloured notes,
My happiness jar has memories of happy thoughts.

A career to celebrate the little moments are more,
The happiness jar will receive its due with so much more.
Cherishing small moments we have learnt to cheer,
Smiling through life with no room for fear.

I often wonder if I had a sadness jar, would it be full,
As life has a little of everything in equal pull;
There is no denying that the heart has ached for sure,
But I still choose to celebrate with my happiness jar in cheer.

The life scorecard has been distributed in its fair share,
There are complaints but more to be grateful there.
Now I fill a jar for gratitude to thank,
For moments that add to my happiness jar, an emotional bank.

VI. Imagine

'Everything you can imagine is real.' — Pablo Picasso

Imagine a world that is free,
From wars over boundaries and generations of enmity!
Imagine seeing colour for its beautiful charm,
And not from the lens of racism ready to harm!

Imagine all homes being the same,
With uniform bank balances, it will be an admirable frame.
Imagine the words 'rich' and 'poor' are erased,
A new dictionary will have to be phrased.
Imagine a Government that delivers the citizens' right,
The dedicated votes will get their might.
Imagine a world not defined by religion,
gender, education, class or a hurtful past,
Can you feel the peace at last?

Imagine a world safer for women we ask,
However modern, this seems like an ambitious task.
Imagine saving the planet as a world as one,
A campaign to dream, sure to stun!

Imagine animals having the gift of speech,
There will be so much for them to teach.
Imagine a world where death knocks on the doors of the very aged,
A fulfilled life lived for all, it's better staged.

Imagine a planet that is clean inside out,
It's not just segregation of garbage that is the worthy shout.
Education for all, empower with care,
Implementing the learning is often a forgotten fare.

Imagine the changing conversations with the world as one,
The society revolutionises and that's no pun.
The news will be read for hope,
Nurturing each other, there is more scope.

With all that we imagine, it is a fragile dream,
Some of it seems futile, to be a unified team.
Improving in small variations, that is possible for sure,
'Change begins with me' a propelling force to cheer.

VII. Time Freeze

'I wish I could freeze this moment, right here,
right now and live in it forever.'
— Suzanne Collins

Sitting in the garden, with a coffee in hand,
Surrounded by my closest people who know
me too well to understand!
There is family and some not related by blood
for sure,
But the bond we made is a lifetime cheer.

It's a bright sunny day; the lush green holds our hearts,
The heartfelt conversations, loud laughter are the only noisy parts.
In the midst of this chaos, there is a calm to preserve,
I yearn for a time freeze; wonder if this is what I deserve!

The breakfast with my mother every Sunday is there,
It's a tradition we stirred with a simple favourite fare.
A morning that reminds me of the forgotten child in me,
A time freeze is needed till eternity.

The soulful conversations with my other half over coffee every day,
On the balcony with the fur baby, a heart-warming tradition at play!
The phone is on silent paying no heed to the world,
A perfect time freeze, everything else is blurred.

Dashing off with these two teens, it's a riot
that I eagerly await,
A girl's soiree, as one would imagine, has
plenty to relate.
Feel like a teen again with them as we chat
like no tomorrow,
This time freeze has me shielded in a bubble
free from sorrow.

With no way to time freeze, it's terrifying
how fast time flies by,
I feel like I am clasping it tight in my hand, a
challenging try.
Then I close my eyes and see the aura of
memories that have shaped,
The happiness is unparalleled, in memories I
am forever draped.

VIII. Criminal Minds

'Scars remind us where we have been. They don't have to dictate where we are going.'
— David Rossi

The lines are blurring and there is no right or wrong,
To the reader this is a peculiar song.
Dressed to kill, or clad in rags, the avatar can be any,
The criminal minds are shaded in forms, so many.

The weapon is an easy tease,
The strategy to kill as they please!
The theft for pleasure, has no room for
reason,
Honesty has disappeared, hello treason.

The money and speed to succeed is the
aspiration,
Oblivious to the means, blinded by the
destination!
The conscience has faded; the shine of power
has invaded mankind,
Amidst criminal minds, saving humanity
must be prioritised.

In a world of good and bad, taking sides is the
easy part,
Cheering the hero or villain, in this life film
chart!
Often the bitter hero, a victim of
circumstance we see,
Becomes the villain with the criminal mind,
fighting one's destiny!

The much-admired hero can be the
much-hated villain in life,
A fine line, hard to stay free from this strife!
This transition can afflict our sanity, causing a
steer,
Balancing this journey, we must adhere.

IX. Last Words

'How lucky am I to have something that makes saying goodbye so hard.' — A A Milne

Known as the keeper of promises, guardian of the English words
In my heart, cherishing moments looking forward!
Living each day as though it's my last,
Making memories that will cherish my past.

The uncertainty of life is a sad reality to all,
It's best to be prepared for the final fall.
If I am faced with an early call to a better place,
My last words should leave a smile on your face.

There have been enough reasons to laugh and cry,
Pacing and embracing life, worth every try.
Milestones that shaped my years' worth a lifetime,
My last words will sing that memory rhyme.

The mind is flustered gauging how to record what I hope to say,
A heartfelt letter, a biography or a soul-stirring poem one day;
A commentary on social media or a creative life play,
My last words will echo to the generation of today.

That excited welcome shriek and the noisy
echo that I make,
No one will hear them; the silence may be
hard to take.
Yet they will remember me with a smile I
hope,
For my madness and spirit, with fondness in
the scope!

The ones closest to my heart, may share a
eulogy to celebrate me,
Hoping I am fondly remembered for eternity.
Etched in my tombstone, the last words will
read,
Make your memories; the heart will follow its
lead.

These are not the lines that define sadness or
agony,
It's the imprint of the unspoken by many.
Death and the end are awkward realities
known to man,
Heartfelt last words will echo character in
this lifespan.

X. Signs of the Times

'The bad news is time flies. The good news is you are the pilot. ' — Michael Altshuler

Times are changing we look around,
Nothing is constant, a reformed life is promised to be bound.
Digital world has eased life is what they say,
Heartfelt conversations are forgotten in this modern day.

Social media is the face of every conversation now,
Our lives are modified to make it 'perfect' somehow.
Every like or share with more friends online to count,
It's the sign of the times, it feels like friendship on discount.

Media and devices are hot buttons that define this frame,
Language in code, scoring with that trending online game!
Retro and nostalgia find its melody in a rare find,
It's the signs of the times with a missing pause and rewind.

Diversity and social injustice, this gen now has a voice to care,
Issues of the social fabric, they are loud but a worthy share.
An opinion so strong, they seek a laudable truce,
It's the signs of the times, connected and impactful with views.

All work and no play is not the mantra today,
A balance of both is here to stay.
Stability, flexibility and world entertainment they seek,
The signs of the times, their life charter have a sorted streak.

Age, gender and social status have no space,
Defining themselves as individuals in the human race!
An opinion so strong, this mini-adult knows more,
The signs of the times, the seniors are struggling, unsure of the life in store.

Superstitions, illogical or forced parenting has no scope,
Unlearning to learn a new approach, to better cope!
Grandma's tales that kept the order at bay,
The signs of the times have a vanishing play.

The mind is finally evolving to find its
pedestal here,
Taboo topics and mental health are
encouraged with cheer.
Filters have changed; conversations are
embracing and sure,
The signs of the times, the outspoken, are
replacing fear.

With the signs of the times, dining tables
have a silence of their own!
It's the generation that weighs practicality
with a click of a phone.
There is much to learn and more to worry in
this 'digital' time,
But every change will see the world
revolutionising with a worthy rhyme.

XI. Life Advice to my Younger Self

'Dear younger self, you have always been enough.'
— Alex Elle

I look into the mirror, seeing the greys,
Where have the years gone, counting nights and days?
It's been a roller coaster with reasons to laugh and cry,
Memories were made, lessons learned, it was a worthy try.

Looking back with no regret, but there is life
advice to my younger self,
Live your life with all your heart without fear
of oneself.
Mistakes should be made and learn from
them,
They are your own, no one else can condemn.

Live in the present, and do what makes you
happy for sure,
Life becomes living with this everyday cheer.
Life advice to my younger self, pursue your
passion with might,
In the end, this will be your best fight.

Looking at the larger picture, don't forget the
small wins,
Realise your worth and don't pay heed to
everyone's opinions.
Live in the present and build your character,
Life is like a film from the beginning,
embrace the actor.

Working hard with diligence and
commitment to being honest,
Look beyond yourself and speak up for causes
even in protest.
There is a world that seeks the change from
you,
Dear younger self, humanity is yours, preserve
your virtue.

Failure can be a hurdle at any time,
Reset and move forward with the same
confident rhyme.
The mantra to my younger self I share with
care,
Live, love, and laugh every day, it's a full life
affair.

In this quest of life, make every moment
count,
Don't forget to live your life on any account.
There is a whole life ahead to worry about a
future in store,
Every little experience is required for your
core.

Today I look back and with gratitude I say,
For every version of myself that has been at
play.
I want to thank each version for not giving up
on me,
I am here because of this guarantee.

XII. Day Dream

'The future belongs to those who believe in the beauty of their dreams.' — Eleanor Roosevelt

Am sitting in the coffee shop, that overlooks a football game,
Sitting beside me is my fur ball, with the burger being his only aim.
The beats of the music playing lifts my mind,
It's a happy pause, a perfect unwind.

At that moment, I felt calm,
As I stared into the space; with so much charm,
It's the maze of my day dream now,
An unforgettable dream somehow.

I see my family united beyond life,
Free from animosity and no room for strife.
Two worlds have met, much to exchange with
care,
This day dream should never end is my scare!

Another episode is set in tune,
Sitting by the sea, connected to the glory of
the moon.
I share my heart with stories of another time,
This dream is simple and has a pleasant
rhyme.

The coffee is served with a smile,
My day dream yearns to prolong, all so
worthwhile.
Am back to the chaos, the endless demands
on the phone,
These mental escapes revive the beauty of the
unknown.

XIII. Don't Cry

'People cry not because they are weak. It's because they have been strong for too long.'
— Johnny Depp

The missed deadline, the failed exam or the burnt dish,
Don't cry now we are told, there is a life to cherish.
The little pieces that shatter every day,
Seems to hold our heart in an odd way!

The big heartbreaks, the unimaginable losses
that hurt,
They seem almost unbearable, impossible to
avert.
"Don't cry," they say, "seek the erudition with
care,"
The endless tears from life's trials are difficult
to repair.

The young man, gripped with pain inside,
Being resilient, hiding his tears under a false
pride.
The broken woman will not hold her tears,
The man shielding her grief, braving his fears!

The gender can be any, let no one define,
Your eligibility to cry, will not diminish the
shade of its design.
The heart is in pain, it sees just the human
hurt,
Man or woman, forget the stereotypes that
exert.

The world is changing, connected and ready
to express,
Stories are weaved; there is a façade to
impress.
Society has definitions that must evolve with
time,
Change the formula of 'don't cry' to a
universal rhyme.

XIV. Flawless

'Our existence would be an exasperating shade of gray if we were all flawless.'
— Agustina Bazterrica

The landscape looked green and lush,
It was the beauty of this canvas after a rain
with a charming blush.
There were bright attractive flowers blooming
here,
The flawless garden blended the weeds with
its extravagant cheer.

The eye captures the shades of green,
So much beauty than one has ever seen.
I see the whole that makes the story for me,
It's flawless to my heart till eternity.

In a little cottage by the stream I see,
A family gathered for a meal with glee
It was not a fancy fare for sure,
But a flawless celebration of a memorable occasion with cheer!

Poised with grace but smeared with mud on her face,
The beaming smile radiated through the chaos of the space.
The warmth she showered to welcome the strangers with care,
It was a flawless beauty often lost in the appearances fare.

She was impecunious, but had a character
that was magnanimous for sure,
Suppressing those struggles and pains behind
a selfless cheer!
She laced the room with her little gestures
and devotion,
Her flawless work was magic in motion.

Chasing the Aurora Borealis at night or
talking to the moon,
Experiencing the magic of sunrise or escaping
into the sunset soon.
Sparkling with the magical clear lakes and
seas with worthy colours at play,
Gazing into nature's canvas for its flawless
display!

XV. Advice to my Older Self

'Youth is the gift of nature. But age is a work of art.' — Stanislaw Jerzy Lec

Time has gone by; the greys have taken over,
Changed in shape and size, my document says I am older.
Wrinkles have dawned on me; it's the age I know,
My older self has experiences to share; a worthy show.

My gait has slowed; my health is no longer the
powerhouse it used to be,
Aches have become the force of my core,
perhaps till my living tree.
My eyesight yearns to see the world; the
spectacle is a must,
My older self will eat with care, my favourites
must adjust.

I have slowed down, my mind is not as clear,
I must be patient with myself, and face my
fear.
Times change and patterns are more complex
for sure,
I must be ready to seek help without losing
any cheer.

Check-ups and staying active is the way to be,
Staying busy with the mind and body is the
best guarantee.
Believe in myself and don't wait for the right
time,
Now is the moment, listen to your heart
chime.

The next generation has limited time,
Lending me their ear may not be their rhyme.
Walking alone may be the need of the hour,
Comfortable in my company, reality may be
sour.

There will be times when no one understands
you,
Don't be disheartened, it's perhaps a different
set of view.
As you look ahead to the glory in your silver
years,
Embrace pride and let go of any regret that
appears.

Optimism and kindness, you deserve them
always,
Continue chasing your dreams with passion
and grace.
Leave no room for excuses with ignorance
and the unknown,
This is your life; own it, for you have sown.

I may be older but it's not the end,
My enthusiasm, spirit, and heart will
comprehend.
Any limits that come my way at that time,
Will not hamper my love for life so sublime.

There will be changes that unsettle my mind,
It won't be easy but futile to expect a rewind.
Realise your worth, embrace the future with
grace and a smile,
That will be a dependable anchor at my last
mile.

XVI. The Eulogy I will miss

'We may not be able to witness our own eulogy but we're actually writing it all the time, everyday.'
— Arianna Huffington

The silence is deafening, I wonder what they think,
There is a deep sadness filled to the brink.
Family and friends from far and wide,
Have come together to celebrate my life's tide.

This is about my passing, the ode is rare,
People around me wonder, how can I care?
It's my eulogy, that sparks the interest the most,
After my passing I will miss this toast.

In my eulogy, I hope they say,
She lived with greatness in every way.
A keeper of promises with equations that balance with care,
She loved with her heart, in her unique fare.

She celebrated life and burst with enthusiasm the most,
An eye for rare finds, with peace at the coast!
Friendly and helpful, to the best that she could,
Surprising gestures, which did the world a lot of good!

She loved the words crafted with care,
Poetry and essays, found prowess with her literary fare!
Walking on four, her heart beat for dogs so dear,
The connection was inexplicable, only she knew their tears.

A believer of integrity, she stood for the right,
Friends, family or strangers, it was a clear fight.
With patience she weaved her life with care,
As a mother, daughter, sister, wife and friend so rare!

At that time I wonder who will speak for me,
Words about me, from my friends or family!
Will they struggle to capture my eulogy then?
Or will they bid farewell to me without any words to pen.

In my lifetime, I have written about everyone I care,
It was a literary journey with emotions that pair.
A glimpse into my eulogy, a preview I dreamt to capture for sure,
If mine ceases to happen, at least I had the opportunity to craft this with cheer.

XVII. Fear of Rejection

'Don't let the voice of others' opinions; drown out your own inner voice.' — Steve Jobs

The clock is ticking; it's time for the test,
The heart is pounding, not a moment to rest.
Acceptance is a pressure with no one to spare,
The weight of this word feels like a war ready to declare.

The fear of rejection, lames every reason,
It's a feeling of the unknown, coated with depression.
Being accepted is a victory with pride that speaks,
Overshadowing being rejected, a fabric of the losing streak!

This fear of rejection often holds one back,
Avoiding the opportunity, hiding what one may lack.
It's a scare that clouds our judgement for better use,
The dipping confidence feels like a devil's ruse.

In a world of complex human emotions we see,
Rejection is just one opinion that cannot define our eternity.
Lessons learnt; time to reset the mind,
It's a life philosophy, etched in our hearts we must remind!

It’s a mind game seeking a strategy that will shine,
Unknown of tomorrow, but making the effort should be the punchline.
The fear of rejection will hurt a little for sure,
But the pain of regret, for not attempting will haunt with no cure.

XVIII. Gallery of my Heart

'Have a heart that never hardens, a temper that never tires and a touch that never hurts.'
— Charles Dickens

The invitation read, the opening of an art gallery,
Viewings by an artist so vivid and a showcase of Valery!
There are some captures that resonate with our heart,
There are others which bewilder us from the start.

As I pondered over my planned visit to the show,
I mused about a gallery of my own that I know.
It's the concealed gallery of my heart,
A sacred space with a limited invitation to access this part!

Shades of laughter, tears with memories from many years,
A facet as divine as there were moments of strengths and fears!
There are captures of heartbreaks, joys, hopes and dreams,
It's a gallery unlike any other themes.

With access to only a few that I know,
This gallery is guarded by my mind in tow.
Some parts locked away, while others kindle the nostalgic flow,
Remembering each part, I find my glow.

As life goes on, more to be added to this
space,
While preserving its fragility in this life race!
In equal share, we store every emotion that
comes our way,
In happiness or sadness, this gallery has a
permanent stay.

As I share a preview of my heart's gallery
here,
I am grateful for this memory gallery with
cheer.
I will continue to limit the access with care,
Unconditional and unique, it's my own
eternal fare.

XIX. The Momentary Applause

'The applause of silence is the only one that counts.' — Alfred Jarry

The accolades are many, a milestone has come,
Pride and happiness is an echo for some.
The buzz is gripping, the news is shared,
A picture message displays all that is fared.

The news in the papers garners much praise,
I feel numb and unaffected by this phase.
In my zone, incognito I aspire to be,
My heart is content with this journey of mine
till eternity.

In this time of social posts we see,
The news is viral; friends and strangers are a
community.
The façade so strong, the reality is a fading
myth,
There is a short-lived applause, moving on
herewith.

The likes and shares on social media may seem
the best,
But knowing friends real from reel is the
ultimate test.
If you crave the applauds along the way,
Cherish the cheer of your inner circle, truly
genuine any day.

The recognition is a vice to most,
Who confuse this glory with a fine toast!
I choose my silence; I don't want the news,
My invisibility to the world is what I choose.

I seek no honour and fame in this life,
I yearn for a peaceful journey free from strife.
I will pursue with passion every word I share,
Hoping to inspire and be inspired along the way.

XX. Make a Choice

'May your choices reflect your hopes, not your fears' — Nelson Mandela
ILLUSTRAION NEEDED

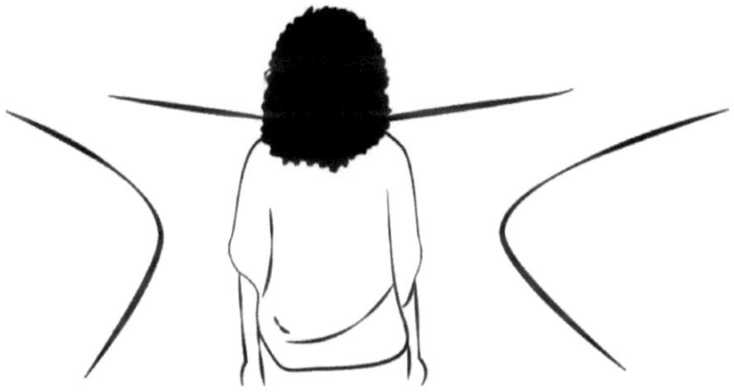

The material splurge or a lifelong equation for
a perfect dream home,
The priority as an individual or a family
anchor in colour or monochrome!
Make a choice of the life that blends in your
vision frame,
It's a weighted journey, be thoughtful and
claim.

A home full of possessions instead of a
passport of experiences we hope,
Nurturing self-growth; as I prepare for the
unknown life scope!
This seems frivolous to many I know,
Making a choice like this has implications
that follow.

Every action has a consequence, so do the
choices we make,
A monumental responsibility, with so much
at stake.
The life we dream, has its own epiphany for
which we prepare,
Make a choice that is your own, with no room
for despair.

When we accept to choose, there is always
something missed,
A dilemma of wonder, it can no longer be
wished.
In hindsight, the choices will logically calm
the confused mind,
Ultimately in consensus, an assurance we
must remind.

Embrace to engage or not, make a choice that
you can own,
Shielded by safety, we lean towards the
familiar zone.
Risks are many, navigate through life and
seize the moment,
In a society so complex, voice your heart or
choose to be silent.

The choices we make reflect the meaning of
life we lead,
Independent choices while dodging the
immediate distracting feed.
Favour that rightfulness than be swayed by
conformity,
Your values will echo the choices we make, an
underestimated enormity.

XXI. Sirens in the Distance

'No siren did so ever charm the ear of the listener as the listening ear has charmed the soul of the siren'. — Henry Taylor

From our home, we could hear,
The faint sirens in the distance, with fear;
It was not the police that loomed our hearts,
The siren of the ambulance kindles our
dreadful pasts.

It was a winter night, down memory lane,
After the world had welcomed the New Year
with parties and champagne;
A health setback no one could imagine,
Rushed in an ambulance, to get a priority
examine.

The flickering light and the sounds so strong,
The stress was pounding in my family's heart
imagining everything wrong.
Unsure about what tomorrow had in fold for
us,
The anxiety was palpable, everything seemed
worthless.

I did receive the care in time,
Next few months, the doctors had an unsure
rhyme.
Recovery made its way to our door,
There was light at the end of the tunnel for
sure.

But long after the hospital episodes were
done,
The siren in the distance fades away any
stroke of fun.
We pray for the safety of the patient
transported in there,
Battling the traffic, I hope they quickly get
the required care.

The sounds of the siren in the distance,
Echo in their hearts like an unforgettable existence.
Did these sounds break their optimism to the core?
A collateral damage amongst so many, an unfathomable score!

This sound could be the emergency vehicle or outdoor warning to hear,
Stay appraised, it's not the sound of cheer.
Mythology associates the sirens with the call to lure the sailors to their deaths,
Every association, we hold our breaths.

The siren in the distance is the sound of our past,
Never forget that it is sure to last.
It reminds us of gratitude, and cherishing every day,
Momentary changes, life is uncertain in every way.

XXII. Sound of Silence

'Silence isn't empty, it's full of answers' – Anonymous

Sitting with a shy demeanour, a glitter in her eye,
Singing like the nightingale and watching the night sky.
She can't hear her song or hear our applause so loud,
Her ears have blocked the world, but she lives her life without doubt.

The onlooker looks at her with a pitiful gaze,
In awe of the melody she creates, a visual sure to amaze.
Every melody note she sang with ease,
Her expression reflected the emotion laced with a subtle tease.

When there is silence, there is calm,
The stillness binds the universe and has its own charm.
The silence here doesn't indicate it's numb,
The attached emotions surface, sometimes louder than the drum.

In this silence, a hug shows the care,
While the tears make it a sad fare!
The echo of silence broadcasts the loud laughter with joy,
The frown on the face gives glimpses of the human annoy.

The silence cherished by some is deafening by most,
The communication is not limited, it has its own method to coast.
The heart is not mute; the signs are speaking to me,
The sound of silence is sailing its own dignity.

In silence, often so much can be said,
More impactful than the cluttered sounds of the words shared.
In the beauty of silence I etch my hope,
To keep my calm with sanity, forever I cope.

XXIII. Teenage Power Shift

'Telling a teenager about the facts of life is like giving fish a bath.' – Arnold Glasow

The ripped loose jeans or clothes in neutral shades,
Black, white or grey, with a look that fades!
The skin care discussions, the changing skincare regime,
The language is so brief, one would question their self-esteem.

The rolling of eyes over the advice that seems
like a rant,
The argument over discipline, it's not an easy
chant.
The emotional outburst over the smallest
nudge,
Tread with care; these humans are hard to
budge.

The emotions shift rapidly from high to low,
Once cheerful will quickly change to an anger
show.
A young child, aching to be an adult in this
age,
At the crossroads of growing, meet the
emotional teenage!

Intense emotions are witnessed as the brain
senses change,
As the teen learns to express and process the
emotional range.
The confusion looming can create sparks of
true sadness,
Or the unwanted anxiety can creep in, staging
awkwardness.

Device specialists, social media experts for sure,
Their faces in a photograph, so devoid of cheer's glow.
The short attention span in the social landscape,
Music and reels are the immediate escape.

Aesthetic and cool is how they want to see their space,
With ideas and aspirations they are following a different race.
The mind is beyond their age to define,
Chosen independence and unique identities is how they refine.

While the mind and body confuse the formula here,
The social saga has its own definition of cure.
Space, new activities is the need of the hour,
Facing their emotions, brace them to empower.

In this complex time, strong role models will
be the best fit,
Patient parents and empathy from the inner
circle balanced with wit.
Mindfulness as a practice reaps benefits for
the teenage years,
It's a mantra that will positively drive away
the fears.

The big changes inside out are the advent of
an era here,
Talking, listening and staying connected are
the best cheer.
Mental health is now defined as a problem for
teenagers,
Changing conversations with these young
adults is a must to remember.

Be the change you hope to be,
Inspire as a role model that impacts
humanity.
Share the purpose; hold the torch with hope,
Make humans that matter with a mind to
cope.

XXIV. Body Positivity

'You define beauty for yourself; society doesn't define your beauty."' — Lady Gaga

The aspirations for the perfect shape,
I am yearning to be the superhero in the cape.
There is a world that defines how I look and feel,
But I look in the mirror and I have nothing to conceal.

A flashback to the time when social media had no space,
Everything was simpler, but judgments were hard to face.
A torture for so many ruffled with the sore of appearances in the past,
A childhood tarnished, it's a heart-breaking broadcast.

From the lean frame in my teenage years,
When life was filled with excitement and free from fears!
There was an abundance of acceptance to my build I know,
I was ignorant of the ones who looked healthy, the mind was weary though.

Years later, I have grown in mind and body I do realise,
The journey has been remarkable, much to my surprise.
Every shape and size I admire and cheer,
Embracing the self, the heart has more value here.

Without reservations, I dress for my mind,
To grow as a person, and let go of every
negativity behind!
When the heart smiles with happiness
anytime,
It's true beauty inside out, truly sublime.

No longer are certain clothes reserved for the
lean few,
Being healthy is what matters, there is a
changed view.
Progressive minds find what matters the
most,
The loving heart and intelligence, wins the
toast.

Body positivity is a philosophy that is a
worthy frame,
Every shape and size is admired regardless of
society's defame.
The mind now sails in optimism and
confidence for many I know,
The heart is content; the society applauds this
image as a worthy show.

Minds are changing; fashion has embraced
this revolution,
Body positivity is now a must in every
resolution.
It's time to block out the shadow of negativity
that looms,
Inclusivity is the way one blooms.

XXV. An Ode to my Inspiration

'I can imagine no heroism greater than motherhood.' — Lance Conrad

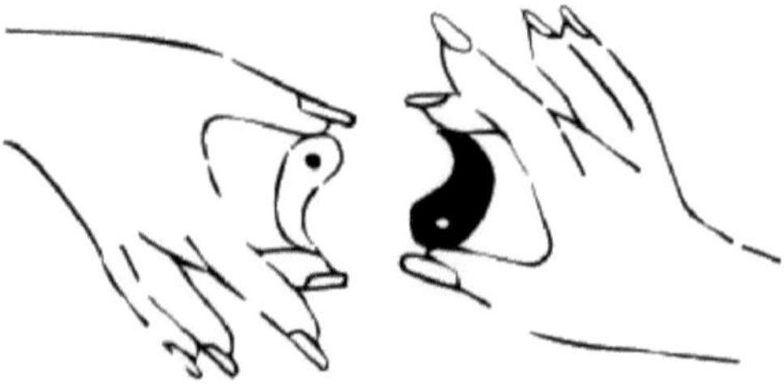

In the mirror, we are two people for sure,
Most find me looking like a reflection of you here.
In many ways this was meant to be,
Forever your shadow, grateful for the inspiration till eternity!

We are alike yet different for sure,
We each have our strengths and flaws here.
Weaved together in an imaginary fabric of hope,
Our lives entwined, we tread this path in life scope.

There is a memory of places we have seen,
Around the globe with experiences that are serene.
The hearty laughter that echoes with every moment of fun,
A travelogue for the reader, but a life memory that can't be forgotten!

Growing up with an anchor so strong,
The lines were clear from right and wrong.
The equation had transpired from perfect parenting to a friendship so strong,
A role model in my eyes, worthy lyrics for a song!

Life experiences have shaped our journey with care,
We are cautious but live with zest beware.
There are many reasons to laugh, cry, and perhaps rage,
Every reason for heartbreak had milestones to balance in exchange.

Today the fraternity speaks of you as strong and brave,
These words echo with every capture in this celebration wave.
A beacon of hope, an inspiration to most,
A worthy mention to applaud with a toast!

Many roles that have been adorned in this life play,
The balance is an adventure, nurturing along the way.
Losses were many; misfortunes rang the bell too often,
But the optimism thrives while the determination is not forgotten.

Today we laugh, cry and speak about our yesterdays with grace,
Always reminding me of blessings, you power a strong embrace.
In this journey of caution and complex human facades,
You have evolved into a resilient woman, refusing to be scarred.

You are modern yet traditional, rigid yet fluid
in ways,
A global view yet a champion of Indianness
stays!
A dreamer yet practical, generous yet careful,
Embracing yet pertinacious, while being
adventurous and experimental!

Just like everyone would idolise their mother
with care,
I hold you on this pedestal while your journey
is a worthy share.
You are not perfect, I accept being true to my
heart,
But your imperfections too shape every part.
We have both grown with time,
Grateful for this equation, truly sublime!
Holding you close, my mother inspires
everyone in many shades,
In my heart truly timeless, one that never
fades!

XXVI. The Gender Story

'Men & Women have roles. Both the roles are different but their rights are equal.' — Harri Holkeri

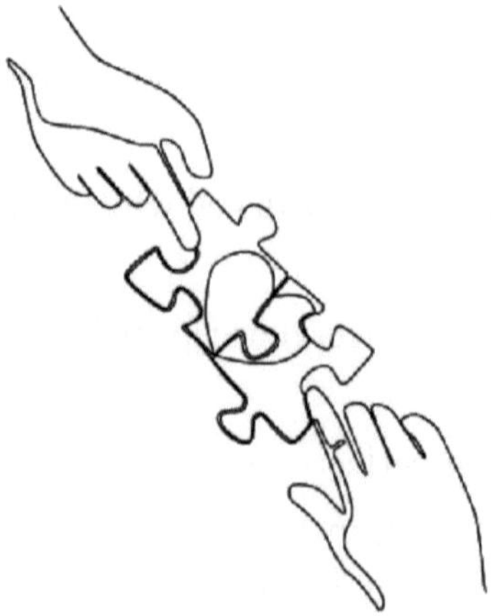

The man and woman debate is endless for sure,
Traits of the gender are prominent here.
Yet the unity of marriage, brings us as one,
So men are from Mars, women are from Venus is no pun.

The right and left of the brain is another
matter,
The man and woman react differently to an
everyday hatter.
Emotional matters may not always be crafted
with care,
Each gender has a stronger gene of an aspect,
to be fair.

Surprises, dates, numbers seem to be a
forgotten script,
Expectations have vaporised, a changed
approach must be equipped.
Multitasking is a dream for most,
A routine and method is the best way to
coast.

A strong body does not mean a strong mind,
Women can balance the emotional roller
coaster grind.
Sensitivity and compassion is not the flavour
here,
But dependability and passion link both with
cheer.

Arranged or love, marriage is when the story starts
Perfectly imperfect, yet an adventure in many parts!
It's a complex story, embarked on a hope,
Each other's presence and absence matter in this scope!

Calm on the face, a smile with charm,
Dapper in fashion, with a strong arm!
An eye for detail, diligent and focused here,
A hearty laughter is rare but affectionate with cheer.

A serious demeanour to the onlooker for sure,
Can be misunderstood for his silence though truly mature!
The mind is often wound up in matters of professional account,
With care and tact, the stressful moment sees a calm turnaround.

Pennywise on a daily note,
Generous beyond understanding, a spiritual devotee, a rare quote.
Grounded yet an occasional pride takes wings,
Confusing to many, but it's the simple things.

A true partner and companion, the praise is right,
Dependable and loving to all his might.
Built with patience, a jubilant trait I cherish,
Injected with the healthy living mantra, an inspiration to nourish!

The praises are many, but his imperfections balance for sure,
Listening selectively treads the daily endure.
Listening in silence is not in him,
Quick to give advice on a whim!

Being calm is an everyday share,
But the anger outbursts have their own repair.
Amused with my enthusiasm and zest for life,
My noisy quirks and celebrations are embraced without strife.

Feels beyond his age, a trait I cannot gather,
Cautious to an extreme, a paranoia rather;
Unbearable to some, but when accepted with grace,
Struggling but efforts are made to ease this trace.

A small circle is shaped with trust,
A difficult nudge to expand if you must;
Traditions, obligations are words that are etched with care,
Weaving this fragility, a character so rare!

A journey so unexpected it has been,
Highs and lows, in all shades we have seen.
Living, loving, learning for more,
With laughter and tears it's a top score.

A lifetime bond is what we yearn,
Grateful for the memories we earn.
We both shape our lives with an unsaid anchor for each other,
A lifetime to tread, together with one another!

XXVII. The Silent Thief

'The time is always right, to do what is right.' — Martin Luther King Jr

In the still of the night, the shadow appears,
The roads are lined with dim lights, yet there are jitters.
The silence is gripping and the soft hush makes it way,
The silent thief emerges to take your soul away.

There is a cloaked man standing with rage,
With the vision of Grim Reaper, the scared heart is unable to gauge.
As I peeped through the window, hoping not to be seen,
The heart is pounding watching this silent thief, a Halloween scene.

In a deserted town with nothing to steal,
I wondered about his reason to appear, perhaps a deal.
A soul for the night is what he may ask,
The silent thief has a horrifying task.

Fate has a similar role to play,
It doesn't see the gender, social status or age on any day.
When destiny knocks and it's time to exit the world,
From rags to riches the report is the same, your time is reserved.

The silent thief emerges without any warning
for sure,
It's the unwanted guest which is accompanied
by no cheer.
While fate has a different life play,
The silent thief of our daily life has its own
way.

In life another silent thief does exist,
The deliberations and procrastination that
often persist.
The indiscipline that we allow to seep into
our lives,
Becomes the silent thief of our time,
irreversible, however hard one strives.

The mind and body often become the target
of the silent thief,
The sudden loss of eyesight or bone loss with
glaucoma and osteoporosis brings medical
grief.

The mental health gets depleted with stress,
A silent thief creeps up to depress.
The grief from unbearable losses and life dismay,
Has a shadow of gloom that is a bitter relay.
The silent thief of grief can sneak into the heart,
Without trying, refusing to part!

Loneliness has an echo that empties the soul,
It's a deep fall, to climb out of this hole,
This silent thief rattles the mind for sure,
Takes away a life of companionship and every ounce of cheer!

We often second-guess our own self-esteem,
Comparison around, it's a life hard to redeem.
Find your centre, be your own,
In this journey, aspire to be the queen of your throne.

Seize the moment; take back your life,
Paint your own destiny, free from unwanted strife.
Make no room for the silent thief to take the space,
Your heart will applaud the effort in this race.

XXVIII. Traditions – Building Cultures

'Cultures grow on the vine of tradition.' – Jonah Goldberg

Traditions are so many, differing by each culture for sure,
Nurtured with care and celebrated with cheer.
Crafted by generations gone by,
Some are evolving with the new minds seeking to fly!

Debate by the youth, should we follow the traditions now,
Often confused about the method somehow;
Often the traditions seem like a complicated fare,
Yet serves an intricate fabric weaving generations so rare!

Pursuing certain traditions blindly I must object,
Devoid of logic and happiness, it needs a true introspect.
What worked for a certain generation, may be of value,
But if dated today, it's time to modify it in my view.

There is a fear of the traditions fading with time,
Society is complex and the youth spin a different rhyme.
Connections have changed and definitions have evolved,
Is it possible to mould these fading traditions with their meaning being dissolved?

I am at the crossroads of two generations that exist,
My elders have passed a legacy, with a hope to persist.
My children are aspiring to be change-makers for a country free of sorrow,
I hold the beacon of hope, blending yesterday and tomorrow.

Many believe that tradition can hinder the progress we dream,
Viewed as a cliché, but also seen as an endless historic theme.
Holding hearts together, building nations is what we believe,
Gustav Mahler echoes the words 'Passing the flame and not preserving the ashes,' are viewed as the key to achieve.

It’s a struggle to stay rooted in this changing landscape,
Tradition and culture have a modern blend, a confusing shape.
I aspire to keep the connection to tradition with the hope,
That the future generations find their own connection in this scope.

XXIX. Goodbye

"My father didn't tell me how to live; he lived and let me watch him do it." Clarence Budington Keland

The flickering lamp struggles to glow but with a fade blur,
It seemed like a farewell was planned and the emotions were clear.
The flame brightens and then disappears with a faint smoke in the air,
It's an unsaid goodbye, expressed with much care.

The words are planned but the speech cannot be delivered,
The heart is heavy, every moment is being remembered.
The fading sight reminds me that I can't hold on,
Like sand through my fingers, it's quickly gone.

There were so many words to be said,
To express my gratitude and life goals ahead!
I yearned to have more time to carve a niche of our bond,
Life passes by unannounced, in my mind it dawned.

Promises were made but I wondered about them,
It felt wrong to ask me for this commitment, an action I condemn.
Did I comply because he was saying his goodbye with ease?
Taking this promise and going with peace.

I hoped to speak to him about my vision for tomorrow,
Making a difference for a country free from sorrow!
I hoped to make him proud of me,
An unfulfilled desire, stretching into eternity.

As I stood there I watched his loved ones around him,
The final moments were here, every chance was dim.
The beats of the devoted music triggered every tear,
Tomorrow without him dawned with fear.

Ironic to bid him goodbye on Father's Day,
To my dad, whom I hoped would stay.
That afternoon, in peace he lay in bed,
Closing his eyes, imagining kindred spirits instead!

He breathed his last; it shredded my heart that day,
Many emotions unfolded within me, it was a harsh play.
Destiny could not be questioned and neither could I ask my dad,
I bid goodbye in silence, with a heart so mad.

Today I look back and remember the scroll I crafted for him,
For Father's Day, when we celebrated and cried, an odd hymn.
As I said goodbye to my teenage saga at 19 that year,
I bid goodbye to his body, keeping him with me, as a memory here.

XXX. Numbness of Being Helpless

'You can only get hurt so much before you get numb.' – Teresa Giudice

In the still of the night, I sat and watched the horror on the screen,
The television was reporting an attack that no one had seen.
It was a story of terror and the moaning cries of the victims there,
That night still echoes in my heart with scare.

This was not the first time the news had such
a sad story to share,
Neither would it be the last one that left the
viewer feeling unfair.
The news of knowing someone in that
treacherous night,
It darkened my heart; my numbness was a
sorry plight.

It was a horror of an almost citywide attack
that was seen,
The victims would be scarred for surviving
the loss that had been.
There was struggle, ruthlessness and
helplessness that was heard,
The valour of the defence was a story that left
us floored.

Every location that witnessed the bloodshed
that night,
I could feel my heart shrinking with the sight.
The pulse of that city had always impressed
me for sure,
Left with a numbness now, sitting afar, and a
raging tremor!

Lives were lost while survivors were shaken beyond repair,
Sitting in front of the television I felt inconsolable despair.
Questions were many, how did the Country witness this night,
When security is applauded, ready for a tough fight!

Three days of struggle and gunshots echoed everywhere,
The remains of the struggle surfaced and martyrs in their coffins were there.
Emotions, fright, and suffering had dented their soul,
But relentless in spirit, the city came together as a whole.

Lives went back to the same chaos and grind,
The scars of the night will always remind.
The numbness injects a shiver unlike any other,
Justice was sought in the eyes of every mother.

XXXI. Strength of a Woman

'Strong women don't have attitude, we have standards.'
— Marilyn Monroe

The silhouette is elegant while she appears fragile,
She dawns grace in her movement and with poise at every mile.
Her delicate appearance can be misconstrued as her weakness,
But the strength of a woman is vested in her uniqueness.

With dreams radiating, every career has a
fighting race,
With compassion in abundance, she balances
the pace.
She holds the torch to build a family while
making her own,
The strength of a woman is often unknown.

With endurance and empathy, a society is
weaved with care,
Her creativity and multi-tasking strength is a
worthy share.
With patience she aims to perfect every role,
The strength of a woman is the optimism that
defines her soul.

Fluid in thought, she adapts to any situation
that may be,
Sensitivity to people and the circumstance in
variety;
Self-assured with healthy boundaries, she will
not be pulled down,
The strength of a woman is endless, befitting
a true 'woman of a woman substance' crown.

Integrity and humility test her journey through life,
With the willingness to forgive, she hopes to keep away from strife.
Her courage is boundless, tested with any despair,
The strength of a woman has channeled emotional intelligence with care.

She will laugh and cry and share her weakness with tears,
She will be able to hold herself together and not be crippled by fears.
Showing emotions is an honest reflection in her eyes,
The strength of a woman will follow her intuition, that's no surprise.

Staying silent is not her trait,
Speaking up at the abuse of power is not her wait.
Don't make the mistake of objectifying our gender,
The strength of the woman is a debate you should surrender.

Don't mistake her tolerance for a lost soul,
She is giving you a chance to refine your role.
Could be outspoken and without a filter one
would say,
The strength of a woman is the creator's
masterpiece at play.

I am a woman, in small measures of what I
define,
I have my flaws that I accept as I refine.
I bear no pride in bearing my soul,
I march towards my destiny, with gratitude in
my life scroll.

XXXII. Laughing Through Tears

Laughter through tears is my favourite emotion'
— Dolly Parton

We sat around the brunch table at noon,
Our voices echoed as our laughter peaked all too soon.
The onlookers from other tables saw our moments of hearty share,
Tears trickled down my cheeks from this uncontrollable laughter so rare.

Such moments we steal for our sanity,
We find peace in happiness ignoring life and its gravity.
It's far and few but added to my memory bank,
Revisiting again when the heart truly sank.

There was a moment back in the day,
One that will forever in my memory stay;
There was looming sadness, for a loved one I had lost,
Confused emotions, we were brimming with exhaust.

The pain was unbearable, I cried in silence, hoping not to be seen,
Wondering about tomorrow without him, I was not keen.
Fate had painted a canvas so bitter for me,
I couldn't see any colour to liberate my mind please.

Amidst that gloom, well-wishers flocked to
express their care,
The condolences felt empty without any
heartfelt share.
They had to be there, at that time,
To mark their attendance in our sadness
rhyme!

A friend sat with me in silence with grief,
From him a friend while from me my brother,
we both lost to an unforgivable thief.
As we spoke about stories of the departed
that were a memory with cheers,
We burst into laughter through the tears.

There were stories that reminded us of happy
days,
We were carefree and away from stressful
ways.
In that moment of grief, the memories gushed
forth with cheer,
For a few moments, we sat there without any
fear.

Laughing through tears felt like the sun on a cloudy day,
In our hearts, all we wanted was for it to stay.
We were looked at with judgement I know,
For smiling in grief, unapproved in that funeral show!

Looking back, I am grateful for that moment we shared,
It helped me reset the loss and helplessness that paired.
It gave me reason to yearn for a life with memories,
Definitely not free, but better braced for worries!

Laughing through tears has a magical portion,
We keep them alive by referring to them as 'is' instead of 'was' on any occasion.
The strength and joy to speak about our departed ones we seek,
Many oblivious to this feeling, feels like a rainbow in the sky so bleak.

Human nature defines sorrow with only tears,
But the innate strength is obtained with that
laughter through fears.
A scene so hard to explain in the face of
adversity,
The mantra we must remind every fraternity.

XXXIII. I Apologise

'Apologies require vulnerability.' — Jennifer Thomas

A note so heartfelt, I write to you,
With honesty, I offer my apology so true.
I have my weakness; I accept it with grace,
I apologise for my limitations, which I must make scarce.

I apologise to my body for the lack of care,
Without exercise and proper sleep in the right share;
Balanced food falls short with the occasional binge,
Junk can be a temptation, an odd cringe.

I apologise to my home for sometimes overlooking your care,
When the grind shreds my patience everywhere;
With dreams of my own I have etched a nest here,
The home routine gets distracted even for this dreamer.

I apologise to the human fraternity who find me wrong,
I cannot apologise for being my own, just strong.
I may offend you when I take a stand,
That's because I believe in my principles, hope you understand.

I apologise to the fur baby who shadows me,
His life begins and ends with me till his eternity.
The anxiety he faces in being out of his sight,
Yet he must learn to face this alright.

I apologise to myself for not being my own,
Hoping to please the world, forgetting what I have sown.
I have my flaws but they make me,
I will own every part that defines my entity.

I apologise for the chaos in my mind,
My promise to better mental health needs this to remind.
I may get drawn to hearsay or unwanted judgement,
Often forgetting my mind is my investment.

I apologise for sometimes not being the perfect fit,
I cannot be contained in a mould or in parts be split.
I see life must have wisdom and folly in its fair share,
Treading this balance always with care!

I have no pride in bearing an apology for sure,
But every apology has my own reflection to hear.
I owe them to my inner self in my time,
My life story is my own script to rhyme.

XXXIV. Being Social on Social Media

'Don't use social media to impress people; use it to impact people.' — Dave Willis

I hear these buzzwords that echo in every domain I know,
The names of different social media platforms are a common show.
The social jargon has changed and the landscape speaks in code,
I need a refresher course, definitely longer than an episode.

This generation with an attention span so short,
A reel is the focus without much thought.
Across mediums, so many tools they find their centre,
It's a different universe; I am a novice, overwhelmed to enter.

The fading question of friends of your own,
Offline we count, but online the world is unknown.
Connections are beyond acquaintances for some,
Friends in a zone or followers seem welcome.

Social interaction is the hope we see,
Across platforms the world is connected online in unity.
The smallest ask, a community to respond here,
Help knocking the door, it's truly a noteworthy atmosphere.

News ripples everywhere, good or bad, a worthy share,
Careers are shaped with the glory of an online stage,
The true introvert is free to engage.

A post is up, the awaited likes, follows and shares is the goal,
Or witness the negative facets of the troll.
The world judges the brevity and snappiness of the post,
Judgement is constant, wanting to please, is the only way to coast.

In the radar but an area of concern for sure,
Cyberbullying has eliminated society in this cheer.
Privacy seems like a luxury of the past,
Unveiling everything online, intruders find their way real fast.

Age is a forgotten fare,
Kids so young are social online everywhere.
Shaping their opinions and moulding them to be like the world we see,
Being your own person is a forgotten identity.

Opinions are strong; sides are taken for sure,
Social issues and awareness have found its solace here with cheer.
Ask for help, need the funds, a word or two,
The miracle of social media will see you through.

An ace behind the camera, so much to say,
Changes rapidly offline, seated mute face to face in dismay,
Conversations have changed, decisions are made,
The future is at stake, from real to reel, it's a fade.

Being social on social media can be a boon or bane,
The looming concern is being able to stay sane.
Gone are the days, when technology had no space,
The world thrived at a different pace.

At the confluence of two generations, I am
finding my way,
With privy to this world yet a stranger to the
social landscape today.
My engagement limits my plug-out any time,
But I cannot chant these words for the next
generation in this rhyme.

XXXV. Sublime Connections to my Roots

'We all carry inside us, people who came before us.' – Liam Callanan

A part of India, almost a world of its own,
Scotland of India, it's always shown.
Coffee, pepper, spices, honey that make their way,
A serene landscape, echoing a peaceful play!

Generations here have found their place,
From royalty or sports not forgetting defence
in the race.
Nestled in a state, but etched with a name of
its own,
Coorg or Kodagu has its roots deeply sown.

Admired with pomp for the weddings
celebrated with cheer,
Unforgettable food, dance, laughter and
abundance in cheer!
Traditions have a complex feel,
An ancestor's blessing, it's a mixed appeal.

The plantations are spread across acres in all
their glory,
Every plant there reflects an almost forgotten
story.
The generation now yearns to stay linked to
the glory of the past,
A culture so strong, it's bound to last.

Farmers or warriors, a stage for both roles,
A combination so unique, blending historic goals!
The family home is the anchor that keeps the culture etched in time,
The offerings and blessings can be sublime.

Family names, an identity and introduction so rare,
The first hello is eased in this fare.
Labour, rain, coffee are conversations in the grind,
The society thrives between fast forward and rewind.

Widely swooned and spoken at length, a worthy applause,
The secret in the food is worth the pause.
Preparations are so unique, a drop of this dark twist,
Blending generations in taste, this cannot be missed.

Achievers are many, icons have made their name,
With roots in the plantation, globally they have changed the game.
The rainforests are a spectacle so divine,
A tourist sanctuary, with hospitality that is known to shine!

The traditional attire has an understated glamour for sure,
Every piece of jewellery and clothing speaks to your core.
The weapons have a legacy that can't be denied,
Debated for its worth, but laced with pride.

Human-animal conflict is a storm that brews here,
The struggle is real, a memorable tourist sighting is not the local cheer.
Shielding the land, both carry the torch of care,
But with no common language, conflict is a scare.

The sounds of the city buzz inside me,
The silence of the plantation landscape is an occasional pause I see.
With a connection of my own to this land that resonates with care,
It will always be my legacy that I hope to share.

XXXVI. Daughters Till Eternity

'In my daughter's eyes, I am a hero. I am strong and wise and I know no fear. But the truth is plain to see, she was sent to rescue me. I see who I want to be in my daughter's eyes.'
— Martina McBride

The soft touch, the gentle care,
Without a nudge, so much to share!
It's not been a long time, but long enough to know,
The affection and warmth radiate a glow.

There is some simplicity with a dash of
teenage rush,
There is life in our hearts, memories we never
want to flush.
Compassion and empathy knows no bounds,
Cherishing the family circle, on any grounds!

Their softness is not their weakness for sure,
They can be strong, silly, independent or
fierce, a perfect cure.
We hope they celebrate their pride, while the
lens of their life should be clear,
Making a difference in life without fear!

With dreams in their hearts, they can aspire
for the moon,
We hope to be the wind beneath their wings
in this tune.
From the playful, innocent, magical world
that they have seen,
With confidence and humility, brace for the
reality in this life scene.

The unsaid words that were always
understood,
A true connection to friendship we have
stood.
There are days when as a parent, we may be
liked less,
For teaching them about life and its mess.

As a parent we see the people they both are
growing to be,
With a heavy heart, we know we have to set
them free.
Holding their hands till the end,
That's a promise to them, with no room to
pretend.

As they embark on a journey of a lifetime,
Become strong yet empathetic individuals at
any time.
Careers and family will have its own place,
We hope they write their own story, it's not a
race.

Blessed with two daughters, couldn't ask for more,
We feel grateful to our core.
Step by step a long way to go,
With milestones and challenges, together we will score.

XXXVII. A Vintage Journey

'The thing about vintage is it never goes out of fashion' — Anthony T Hincks

I walked through a home revived as a vintage museum to share,
Set against the lush green forests surrounded by hills, a scene so rare.
A small stream was flowing near the home,
A picturesque scene, truly magical to roam.

Inside the house were curated vintage finds,
Which fascinated us and transported our minds.
Every artefact seems from a forgotten time,
Memories gushing back, it's a nostalgic rhyme.

The shining cycle rickshaw stood there with panache and charm,
Iconic for its time, it shrieked a bell sounding like a rustic alarm.
The seating housed a covered canopy so rare,
It paced with ease, with a marginal fare.

The Grandfather's clock echoed at the very hour,
Poised with grandeur, it had its own antique power.
True clockwork it performed to the exact time,
It felt like a pause so sublime.

Music echoes from the record player there,
The discs were iconic, black and fragile to
care.
The gramophone had another surprise for us,
This melody echoed an antique greatness.

We turned to see this beautiful dial
telephone,
Where cords were needed to operate on their
own.
Calling the operator to place the call,
It was a much-awaited ring down the hall.

There were other collectables that rang a
unique rhyme,
The iconic sewing machine, a steam iron all
had a classic chime.
A wooden treasure chest, decorated in gold
was set in a room with care,
This collection is much sought after, every
collectable so rare.

The museum was lit with kerosene lamps so rare,
Dimly lit but was glowing in its grandeur fare.
The air carried the aromas of yesterday,
The restless heart was now calm with this familiar day.

This museum painted a canvas so beautiful and pure,
It felt like a revival from every chaos, a rejuvenation tour.
There was a heartfelt welcome and farewell we got,
Everything of the past is a perfect comeback, the kind most sought.

XXXVIII. Today - blending our yesterday & tomorrow

'Learn from yesterday, live for today, hope for tomorrow.' — *Albert Einstein*

Living in my yesterday, I now see the gloom,
I need to let the light into my room.
A new chapter awaits us I know,
It's the story of tomorrow waiting for its show.

The knock on the door of tomorrow is faint,
But the canvas of life ahead is a promising vibrant paint.
Could this be an illusion I wonder in dismay,
Puzzled at the tomorrow that will unfold in this life play!

Every step we take forward, we are sure,
A shadow of yesterday will follow us tomorrow in sadness or cheer.
So look back with the wisdom that life has shown,
Embracing without regret is the best way to have grown.

Looking back I see the person I was yesterday,
Growing as a person, I have come to this day.
There were laughs and tears along the way,
These facets are in my tomorrow, in this tapestry of life it will forever stay.

Who has seen tomorrow one may say,
Yet we live our life like it's our last day.
Live, love, laugh is a philosophy that will shine,
In a world that humanity struggles to define.

XXXIX. Community Matters

'Alone we can do so little; together we can do so much.' — Helen Keller

Step out of my door, waiting for the lift,
We exchange smiles; it has been a recent shift.
Pleasantries are shared, familiarity is built here,
Meeting our neighbours, start of the cheer!

Travel memorabilia or festive treats are being shared,
Thoughtfully given, truly cared.
A welcome meal is hosted to build the bond,
A new connection has been dawned.

Many homes, one community,
The equations are redefined in unity.
Celebrations, festivities, tournaments,
moments of need are all united,
Attendance is prompt, need not be invited.

It's not just the next-door neighbour to boost our day,
Any home in the community is an extended family at play.
Pets have a thriving community of their own,
Kids are enriched with memories sown.

Groups are many at the click of the phone,
Envision an interest and find your zone.
Have a question, or query on the smallest matter,
Quick to respond, more proactive than
Google in this chatter!

The handy tip, the valuable care to try,
Referring to a dependable help or just the
useful spy!
Large communities like any other have issues
of their own,
Arguments can be many, but quickly a
forgotten zone.

An everyday routine, each to their own,
Deadlines and rush hour woes, no one is
alone.
Everyday live in a bubble of your own,
Yet feel connected when it's a community
zone.

Initiatives of social impact, teach the next
generation to care,
Garbage segregation, donations or the
second-hand fair;
A secure space that combines every facet of
our day,
Nothing like home with these neighbours, we
are sure to stay!

Achievements, talents so much promise
thrives here,
Each one has a crown of their own, yet
humility is their cheer.
In M. Angelou's line, 'Community is much
more than belonging to something;
It's about doing something together that
makes belonging matter.'

XXXX. Entitled

'Entitlement is a delusion built on self-centeredness and laziness' — Unknown

The generation is unlike any other we know,
It's an everyday decipher like a complex code.
Parenting is no longer a page from our past,
We need a rewiring for our sanity to last.

In many ways they seem like an entitled bunch,
Basking in their bubble, unaffected by a struggle crunch;
They have a pattern, an expectation of their own,
Almost privileged, as if it were sown!

Parenting has become a learning everyday,
Almost an experiment, the trial and error way;
Equations of hierarchy have disappeared with time,
It's a communication of equals in this new rhyme.

Shaping well-rounded individuals is no cup of tea,
Teaching about life and values is not a one-way street.
A convincing argument and then the point is taken,
Negotiations and bargains are aptly shaken.

Parents and grandparents have seen struggles
of their own,
Values built have with time, grown.
As we nurture a generation blended with
technology and practical know-how,
Yet mental health becomes a fragile facet
somehow.

With this entitled generation, as we find
hacks that we can adapt,
It's a Google universe constantly pushing out
the most apt.
As we move forward with hope and care,
We yearn that this generation kindles
humanity with a perfect share.

XXXXI. Eggs & Bread – food for every season without reason

'Poached eggs are good, poached animals are not'
— Erma Bombeck

Every Sunday morning a tradition so rare,
It's breakfast with my mom, unmatched with care.
She hopes to dish up the exotic finds with her skill,
But the heart yearns for the staple bread and egg, an unforgettable thrill.

An odd perspective for my reader, but the
greatest invention ever known,
Egg and bread, a combination like no other to
be ever shown;
Poached, scrambled, omelettes or boiled if
you may,
My personal favourite, the sunny side up,
makes my day.

Combine that with a bread of your choice,
White, brown, wheat, multigrain, worth every
slice.
Gourmet breads now have found their way,
Handmade without preservatives with
flavours are here to stay.

Egg has the protein boost; a must for our
health,
With balance and flavour, it's the king of food
wealth.
The bread is frowned upon for its dietary
worth,
A little indulgence so worth it, a staple since
birth.

Bread and eggs have a universal appeal,
Travel the world and find your boost with this zeal.
Dished out with surprise ingredients, chanted as the global breakfast brand,
Don't be surprised, lunch and dinner too find this combo truly grand.

Agreed to be the best, my dad and me,
Great minds think alike till infinity.
We both shared the joy for this combination so simple,
Proclaimed by me as an icon of our time, a nostalgic symbol!

XXXXII. Opening the Mailbox

'Nothing echoes like an empty mailbox.' – Charles Schulz

It's a time from another era you may feel,
Eagerly waiting for the postman to appear
and not a cool reel;
I peek out of the window, watching my
mailbox,
He appears with a smile and leaves after he
drops.

I rush to this charming red metallic piece,
With a curve-shaped top, it echoes a classic tease.
Secured with a lock so protrusive,
One would imagine it's a treasure; definitely exclusive.

I open the mailbox and find a bunch of envelopes addressed to me,
These are letters from friends and family away in another city.
Making connections with the vintage handwritten letters we hoped,
A charm quickly fading, we realised we struggled and coped.

A burst of emotions rushed through my mind,
Across the oceans, equations were entwined.
The letters brought news of lives that matter,
There were milestones and heartbreaks, in equal chatter.

There were posts from strangers who became friends,
The occasional pen pals, with worry that everyone contends;
As a writer, I did receive letters from publishing houses that scare,
The acceptance or rejection of a literary piece, always a surprising affair!

I was asked by my neighbours about the convenience of the phone,
They imagined me to be dated in another zone.
Little did they imagine that technology was around me!
But I felt my true connection to the mailbox; a forgotten entity.

XXXXIII. Be a rainbow

Try to be a rainbow in someone's' cloud.' – Maya Angelou

The skies are blue but there is a looming tease,
The sun and the rain are seeking an ease.
Gradually I see the sky painted like a canvas so rare,
The sprawling rainbow is a treat to the eye; an elaborate affair.

The sunlight radiates through the water droplets in the air,
The colours are seven, a rich and memorable glare.
After the beautiful rains, it's like petrichor scented everywhere,
It's now a visual and aromatic treat, a combination so rare.

The clouds sometimes so rough or the rains disrupt the time,
But the joy of the rainbow makes it a worthy rhyme.
Be the optimist who sees the colour in the sky,
Overlook the rain that keeps you complaining about why?

Just like life, today there may be some struggles and sadness to bear,
But the rainbow is like the joy after the hardship to care.
Destiny will have its own cards to play,
Smiling with radiance in the rainbow colours is your own life relay.

Every speck of nature has something that is a page of learning for all,
Find the parts that make your heart beat and ignore a bad call.
Life will give you chances to make that impact on others,
Brighten their life with rainbows than gloom them with tears.

XXXXIV. Childhood dreams

'Childhood is the one story that stands by itself in every soul.' – Ivan Doig

Looking at the treasure chest, I see my childhood peeking at me,
There are stories of a younger me that spell sublimity.
Times were simple and our needs were not much,
Our life story is now weaved with a complex touch.

Transport me back to the days of laughter
and play,
Outdoors were our games, night and day.
The books that we read shared a simple
rhyme,
We didn't need life messages that scared the
school time.

Playtime involved the park or board games on
the shelf,
Time to rewind, gadgets had no space for self.
The teachers' class and the parent's lessons
meant to learn it now,
No room for debate, no questions asked
somehow.

We had dreams that did not go beyond our
neighbourhood or town,
Aspiring for another region was definitely an
unknown crown.
Our eagerness to harness the role of an adult
did prove dear,
It's a one-way journey, there is no returning
here.

Now worries have doubled and stillness is
nowhere to be seen,
Being bored is a forgotten mantra hidden in a
screen.
Yearning for a yesterday with memories that
shine,
This is the flight to tomorrow, nature's design.

XXXXV. The Last time I Danced

'Dance is the hidden language of the soul.'
— Martha Graham

The last time I danced, I swirled with ease,
The movement was free, the body did not tease.
There were beats I could catch without a miss,
It was a younger me, the harmony was bliss.

The last time I danced, I did not worry about the onlooker here,
The heart knew no bounds to my cheer.
Carefree is what I remember I was defined as back then,
Seeking to impress no one, life was a ten.

The last time I danced I could feel the music speak to me,
There were words that charmed my sanity.
I shared the jubilation with those around in the room,
I felt radiant and free from gloom.

The last time I danced, I didn't need to be taught,
Every step was a reflection of what I thought.
Grace by my side, energy to keep a song,
The hours didn't clock, it never felt long.

The last time I danced, I felt as light as a feather,
The soul was charmed, ready to brave any weather.
Life has counted its years and I see my grip has shaken,
But the heart is like when I danced, never forsaken.

XXXXVI. Time for Change

'Be the change you wish to see in the world.'
— Mahatma Gandhi

Nothing is constant, there is bound to change,
Accepting it is in our range.
Defining our tomorrow depends on how we embrace,
The modifications around us with tact and grace!

The world will see this change, technology has evolved now,
Build yourself for a better tomorrow, cope with the change somehow.
Better your skills, find your relevance today,
There are battles in your life play.

As a person I will change with age,
Circumstances and experience brace me to better engage.
The world may not cherish every change I make,
But accepting my strengths and flaws will be the real take.

Life gets better with change is what they say,
Keep your head high and ride away.
Facing change all depends on the mind,
It's up to you if you want to move forward or rewind.

It's a challenge to ride this roller coaster for
sure,
Change has a speed breaker that can dampen
the cheer.
We wake up to a new day, hoping for a better
rhyme,
The change is ours, acceptance makes it truly
sublime.

XXXXVII. Sarcasm - the sorry reaction

"Sarcasm is the body's natural defence against stupidity." — Unknown

Every emotion I can brace,
But the hurt through sarcasm leaves a dark trace.
An odd response in many situations we see,
Feels like a defence but breaks the heart to a large degree.

Coping with sadness or fear, people use sarcasm as a defence,
Hidden behind their own shadow, they overlook the offence.
The heart yearns to be spoken with grace,
Tasteful for sure, often forgotten in the competitive race!

Many pretend that sarcasm radiates humour for sure,
An odd style, but seen with much cheer.
An icebreaker for many, for better stranger conversations,
Where is humanity with their expectations?

The irony is that sarcasm has some notes of distaste in the tone,
There is a closed mind emulating this, though mentally alone.
Read the lines, see the spoken and unspoken here,
Don't miss the traces that are filled with fear.

Sarcasm is a mechanism I am yet to see the
reason,
It’s a hard logic when I am enraged with
sarcasm in every season.
Seek the wise and find the words that charm,
It's music to any ears, free from harm.

XXXXVIII. SUBLIMITY - THE POWER TO INSPIRE

(ACROSTIC POEM)

Shades of colour fill the canvas of life,

Under the chaos of everyday grind, in happiness or strife!

Build your dreams with memories that bring cheer,

Live your life with hopes that are free from fear.

Ideate with yourself and evolve as a person,

Making a meaningful life; all within reason!

Identify every reason that transports you to the past,

Travel to the future, direct your own life cast.

Yesterday holds lessons for a better tomorrow,

Tread with care, caution reduces any sorrow.

Hold your head high and own every decision,

Empower yourself to be your own person.

Perfection has many shades,

Open your mind to embracing feedback and accolades.

Waive the wand of forgiveness with no condition,

Embrace disappointment and accept the apology in your position.

Resolve to share your love and knowledge with one and all,

Thank humanity for the opportunity big or small.

Own your mistakes and change your viewing lens,

Identify your weakness and make necessary amends.

Nurture every equation that is in your circle with care,

Sacrifice is a tall task for humanity so beware.

Practice mindfulness and find solace in your inner core,

Ideal is a vision, be realistic therefore.

Reflect on the life gone by and look with cheer,

Each day is a new one, live like it's your last here!

Printed by Libri Plureos GmbH in Hamburg,
Germany

9 789363 30669